LAST DREAM

LAST DREAM

Giovanni Pascoli

Translated from the Italian
by Geoffrey Brock

WORLD POETRY BOOKS

World Poetry Books

Storrs, CT 06269

www.worldpoetrybooks.com

English translation copyright © 2019 by Geoffrey Brock

All rights reserved

This book is made possible with support from the Stavros Niarchos Foundation.

Library of Congress Cataloging-in-Publication Data

Names: Pascoli, Giovanni, author; Brock, Geoffrey, translator

Title: Last Dream / Giovanni Pascoli.

Description: Storrs, Connecticut : World Poetry Books [2019]

Identifiers: LCCN 2019905462

 ISBN 978-0-9992613-5-4

Published in the United States of America

2 4 6 8 10 9 7 5 3 1

Cover design by Kyle G. Hunter

Book design by Brian Sneeden

CONTENTS

In memory of Umberto Eco

"I didn't know Pascoli," Sibilla said. "Listen
how lovely it is..."

— *The Mysterious Flame of Queen Loana*

from *Myricae*

Patria

Sogno d'un dì d'estate.

Quanto scampanellare
tremulo di cicale!
Stridule pel filare
moveva il maestrale
le foglie accartocciate.

Scendea tra gli olmi il sole
in fascie polverose:
erano in ciel due sole
nuvole, tenui, róse:
due bianche spennellate

in tutto il ciel turchino.

Siepi di melograno,
fratte di tamerice,
il palpito lontano
d'una trebbïatrice,
l'angelus argentino...

Home

Dream of a summer's day...

What a jittery trill
of cicadas! Vine leaves
shrivel and shrill
as the mistral moves
through and away.

Dusty ribbons
of sun among the oaks...
Across the heavens
like white brushstrokes
two faint clouds fray

into the sprawling blue.

A pomegranate hedge,
a tamarisk copse.
A thresher beyond the ridge
that rumbles then stops.
The silvery Angelus, too...

dov'ero? Le campane
mi dissero dov'ero,
piangendo, mentre un cane
latrava al forestiero,
che andava a capo chino.

Where am I? The bells
tell me, mournfully,
as a dog howls
at the stranger as he
passes, head bowed, through.

I puffini dell'Adriatico

Tra cielo e mare (un rigo di carmine
recide intorno l'acque marezzate)
parlano. È un'alba cerula d'estate:
non una randa in tutto quel turchino.

Pur voci reca il soffio del garbino
con ozïose e tremule risate.
Sono i puffini: su le mute ondate pende
quel chiacchiericcio mattutino.

Sembra un vociare, per la calma, fioco, di
marinai, ch'ad ora ad ora giunga
tra 'l fievole sciacquìo della risacca;

quando, stagliate dentro l'oro e il fuoco,
le paranzelle in una riga lunga
dondolano sul mar liscio di lacca.

Shearwaters of the Adriatic

Sky and sea, and somewhere between the two
(a line of crimson edging the marbled water)
they speak. It is an azure dawn in summer
and not a sail in sight in all that blue.

Yet the libeccio blows in bearing speech:
voices and, with them, lazy wisps of laughter.
It's the shearwaters' raucous morning chatter
skittering over swells to the hushed beach.

It sounds, amid that calm, like the faint shouts
of fishermen that sometimes reach the shore
(above the tide's own whispered ins and outs)

when a long line of distant trawlers, blacker
than night against the gold and the far fire,
sits rocking on a glossy sea of lacquer.

Pensieri

a G.S.

II. I TRE GRAPPOLI

Ha tre, Giacinto, grappoli la vite.
Bevi del primo il limpido piacere;
bevi dell'altro l'oblio breve e mite;
      e...più non bere:

chè sonno è il terzo, e con lo sguardo acuto
nel nero sonno vigila, da un canto,
sappi, il dolore; e alto grida un
      muto pianto già pianto.

Five Epigrams

to Giacinto Stiavelli

II. THREE GRAPES

Three grapes, Giacinto, grow upon these vines:
The first is pleasure, and is clear as air;
the next is sweet amnesia. Drink their wines,
    yes—but stop there,

because the third is sleep, in whose dark corner,
keeping a keen-eyed vigil (as you know),
sits grief. And loud is the mute cry the mourner
    cried long ago.

III. SAPÏENZA

Sali pensoso la romita altura
ove ha il suo nido l'aquila e il torrente,
e centro della lontananza oscura
    sta, sapïente.

Oh! scruta intorno gl'ignorati abissi:
più ti va lungi l'occhio del pensiero,
più presso viene quello che tu fissi:
    ombra e mistero.

III. WISDOM

Full of your thoughts, climb to the lonely summits
from which cascades descend and eagles rise,
and there, yourself the center of gray distance,
stand, and be wise.

Ah, study those unfathomed depths around you:
the farther out the eye of your thought strays,
the nearer comes the thing you're staring into:
mystery, haze.

IV. CUORE E CIELO

Nel cuor dove ogni visïon s'immilla,
e spazio al cielo ed alla terra avanza,
talor si spenge un desiderio, e brilla
            una speranza:

come nel cielo, oceano profondo,
dove ascendendo il pensier nostro annega,
tramonta un'Alfa, e pullula dal fondo
            cupo un'Omega.

IV. HEART AND SKY

In the heart, where every vision multiplies
and sky and earth are overwhelmed by space,
a longing may die down, and a hope rise
                up in its place—

the way, in the sky's ocean of deep blue
(where our thought drowns, ascending out of reach)
Alphas may set and, from dark depths, some new
                Omega breach.

V. MORTE E SOLE

Fissa la morte: costellazïone
lugubre che in un cielo nero brilla:
breve parola, chiara visïone:
            leggi, o pupilla.

Non puoi. Così, se fissi mai l'immoto
astro nei cieli solitari ardente,
se guardi il sole, occhio, che vedi? Un vòto
            vortice, un niente.

V. DEATH AND SUN

Gaze upon death: that gloomy constellation
that shines against the blackness of the sky,
that sudden word, pellucid apparition—
                translate it, Eye.

You cannot. Likewise when you gaze upon
the star that in our lonely sky is burning,
you see—what, Eye? A nothingness of sun,
                a void, churning.

VIII. IL PASSATO

Rivedo i luoghi dove un giorno ho pianto:
un sorriso mi sembra ora quel pianto.
Rivedo i luoghi, dove ho già sorriso...
Oh! come lacrimoso quel sorriso!

VIII. THE PAST

Returning to places where I once shed tears,
I see in those tears now a kind of smile.
Returning to places where I used to smile—
oh! those smiles: how full they were of tears!

Allora!

Allora ... in un tempo assai lunge
felice fui molto; non ora:
ma quanta dolcezza mi giunge
da tanta dolcezza d'allora!

Quell'anno! per anni che poi
fuggirono, che fuggiranno,
non puoi, mio pensiero, non puoi,
portare con te, che quell'anno!

Un giorno fu quello, ch'è senza
compagno, ch'è senza ritorno;
la vita fu van parvenza
sì prima sì dopo quel giorno!

Un punto! ... così passeggero,
che in vero passò non raggiunto,
ma bello così, che molto ero
felice, felice, quel punto!

Back Then!

Back then, in those now-distant times,
I was the happiest of men—
no longer. Yet what sweetness comes
still from that sweetness then!

That year! Of all the years now gone,
and all that, soon, shall disappear,
my thoughts shall carry with them none—
none, I say—but that year!

A day is what it was, its brilliance
peerless, and then it slipped away,
rendering life but a vain semblance
before and since that day!

A moment... one that passed me by
before I'd ever really known it.
But that's fine: I was happy, I
was *happy*, in that moment!

Arano

Al campo, dove roggio nel filare
qualche pampano brilla, e dalle fratte
sembra la nebbia mattinal fumare,

arano: a lente grida, uno le lente
vacche spinge; altri semina; un ribatte
le porche con sua marra paziente;

ché il passero saputo in cor già gode,
e il tutto spia dai rami irti del moro;
e il pettirosso: nelle siepi s'ode
il suo sottil tintinno come d'oro.

Plowing

Out in the field, where a few leaves gleam
russet on vines, and the morning mist
lifts from the hedgerows like steam,

they're plowing: one man goads the slow
cows with slow shouts, one sows, one hits
the ridges with his patient hoe—

already the knowing sparrow thrills,
eyeing it all from his mulberry hold;
and in the hedge, the robin, whose trills
are delicate as drops of gold.

La via ferrata

Tra gli argini su cui mucche tranquilla-
mente pascono, bruna si difila
la via ferrata che lontano brilla;

e nel cielo di perla dritti, uguali,
con loro trama delle aeree fila
digradano in fuggente ordine i pali.

Qual di gemiti e d'ululi rombando
cresce e dilegua femminil lamento?
I fili di metallo a quando a quando
squillano, immensa arpa sonora, al vento.

Railway

Between embankments on which cattle
graze calmly, the railway runs until
it's a distant glimmer of brown metal,

and tall poles in file, bearing away
against a pearly sky their airy
weft of wires, steadily decay.

What cries are these that, like a woman's
moaned lament, rise and descend?
Now and again those metal strands—
vast thrumming harp—keen in the wind.

Temporale

Un bubbolìo lontano...

Rosseggia l'orizzonte,
come affocato, a mare:
nero di pece, a monte,
stracci di nubi chiare:
tra il nero un casolare:
un'ala di gabbiano.

Storm

A distant rumbling...

Seaward, the horizon
reddens, as if ablaze;
above the pitch-black mountain
rags of bright clouds;
amid the black a house:
a seagull's wing.

Il lampo e il tuono

1.

E cielo e terra si mostrò qual era:

la terra ansante, livida, in sussulto;
il cielo ingombro, tragico, disfatto:
bianca bianca nel tacito tumulto
una casa apparì sparì d'un tratto;
come un occhio, che, largo, esterrefatto,
s'aprì si chiuse, nella notte nera.

2.

E nella notte nera come il nulla,

a un tratto, col fragor d'arduo dirupo
che frana, il tuono rimbombò di schianto:
rimbombò, rimbalzò, rotolò cupo,
e tacque, e poi rimareggiò rinfranto,
e poi vanì. Soave allora un canto
s'udì di madre, e il moto di una culla.

Lightning and Thunder

1.

Both earth and sky laid bare to sight:

the earth a gasping, livid tremor,
the sky collapsing, tragic, finished—
and blank white in the quiet clamor
a house appeared a house vanished,
like an eye that—aghast, astonished—
widens and shuts, in the black night.

2.

And in the black night's nothing-dark,

a sudden roar like a cliff crumbling,
as a thunderclap booms and splinters—
booming, rebounding, grimly rumbling
away, then washing back in tatters,
then fading. Tenderly now: a mother's
soft song, the creak of a cradle's arc.

Novembre

Gemmea l'aria, il sole così chiaro
che tu ricerchi gli albicocchi in fiore,
e del prunalbo l'odorino amaro
       senti nel cuore.

Ma secco è il pruno, e le stecchite piante
di nere trame segnano il sereno,
e vuoto il cielo, e cavo al piè sonante
       sembra il terreno.

Silenzio, intorno: solo, alle ventate,
odi lontano, da giardini ed orti,
di foglie un cader fragile. È l'estate,
       fredda, dei morti.

November

Gemlike the air, the sun so bright above
you look for blossoms on the apricot trees,
recall the bitter whitethorn scent you love
        and sniff the breeze.

But the whitethorn's withered, the brittle boughs
hatch their black schemes against the empty blue,
and the earth rings hollow now beneath the blows
        of every shoe.

Around you, silence, but for sighs that spill
in upon every gust, from grove and wood:
frail settlements of leaves. This is the chill
        summer of the dead.

Mare

M'affaccio alla finestra, e vedo il mare;
vanno le stelle, trèmolano l'onde.
Vedo stelle passare, onde passare:
un guizzo chiama, un palpito risponde.

Ecco sospira l'acqua, àlita il vento:
sul mare è apparso un bel ponte d'argento.

Ponte gettato sui laghi sereni,
per chi dunque sei fatto e dove meni?

Sea

Through the window, I watch the ocean;
the waves tremble, and the stars rise.
I watch the waves, the stars, their motion:
a flash calls out, a pulse replies.

Listen: the sigh of sea, of wind,
and on the water, a bridge of silver...

O bridge cast over placid water,
who are you here for? where do you end?

In cammino

Siede sopra una pietra del cammino,
a notte fonda, nel nebbioso piano:
e tra la nebbia sente il pellegrino
le foglie secche stridere pian piano:
il cielo geme, immobile, lontano,
e l'uomo pensa: Non sorgerò più.

Pensa: un occhiata quale passeggero,
vana, ha gettata a passeggero in via,
è la sua vita, e impresse nel pensiero
l'orma che lascia il sogno che s'oblia;
un'orma lieve, che non sa se sia
spento dolore o gioia che non fu.

Ed ecco—quasi sopra la sua tomba
siede, tra l'invisibile caduta—
passa uno squillo tremulo di tromba
che tra la nebbia, nel passar, saluta;
squillo che viene d'oltre l'ombra muta,
d'oltre la nebbia: di più su: più su,

On the Road

The pilgrim's resting on a wayside stone,
it's late at night, and mist is on the heath,
and in the distance he can hear the moan
of the unmoving sky, and far beneath
the quiet scrape of leaf on withered leaf—
and he is thinking: I will not rise again.

He thinks: the glance a traveler idly cast
at one who happened by him on his way,
that was his life, and on him it impressed
such traces as a dream leaves on the day—
faint traces of (but who, he thinks, can say?)
a thwarted joy or some forgotten pain.

It's then—with him atop that rock as if
on his own tomb, amid the unseen fall—
that the man hears a ragged, brassy riff
passing above him through the mist: a call
arriving from beyond the muffling pall,
from high above the mist: a higher plane,

dove serene brillano le stelle
sul mar di nebbia, sul fumoso mare
in cui t'allunghi in pallide fiammelle
tu, lento Carro, e tu, Stella polare,
passano squilli come di fanfare,
passa un nero triangolo di gru.

Tra le serene costellazïoni
vanno e la nebbia delle lande strane;
vanno incessanti a tiepidi valloni,
a verdi oasi, ad isole lontane,
a dilagate cerule fiumane,
vanno al misterïoso Timbuctù.

Sono passate... Ma la testa alzava
dalla sua pietra intento il pellegrino
a quella voce, e tra la nebbia cava
riprese il suo bordone e il suo destino:
tranquillamente seguitò il cammino
dietro lo squillo che vanìa laggiù.

where heavenly bodies glimmer calmly forth
over the sea of mist, the murky sea
upon which you project, Star of the North,
and you, slow Wain, your pale intensity—
arriving with a fanfare, a reveille:
a black triangular flock of passing cranes.

Between calm constellations and these strange
mist-covered heaths they fly, toward the highlands
and balmy valleys of their winter range,
the green oases and the far-flung islands,
unceasing, toward the sprawling broad ceruleans
of floodplains—toward the African arcane.

Soon they had passed. The pilgrim at his rest
lifted his head from his wayside stone, intent
upon that voice, and in the hollow mist
took up his staff and his fate again: he went
calm down the road, whichever way it bent,
trailing that call that in the darkness waned.

Ultimo sogno

Da un immoto fragor di carrïaggi
ferrei, moventi verso l'infinito
tra schiocchi acuti e fremiti selvaggi...
un silenzio improvviso. Ero guarito.

Era spirato il nembo del mio male
in un alito. Un muovere di ciglia;
e vidi la mia madre al capezzale:
io la guardava senza meraviglia.

Libero!... inerte sì, forse, quand'io
le mani al petto sciogliere volessi:
ma non volevo. Udivasi un fruscio
sottile, assiduo, quasi di cipressi;

quasi d'un fiume che cercasse il mare
inesistente, in un immenso piano:
io ne seguiva il vano sussurrare,
sempre lo stesso, sempre più lontano.

Last Dream

Out of a motionless infernal
shudder and clang of steel on steel
as wagons moved toward the eternal,
a sudden silence: I was healed.

The stormcloud of my sickness fled
on a breath. A flickering of eyes,
and I saw my mother by my bed
and gazed at her without surprise.

Free! Helpless, yes, to move the hands
clasped on my chest—but I had no
desire to move. The rustling sounds
(like cypress trees, like streams that flow

across vast prairies seeking seas
that don't exist) were thin, insistent:
I followed after those vain sighs,
ever the same, ever more distant.

from *Canti di Castelvecchio*

Nebbia

Nascondi le cose lontane,
tu nebbia impalpabile e scialba,
tu fumo che ancora rampolli,
    su l'alba,
da' lampi notturni e da' crolli
    d'aeree frane!

Nascondi le cose lontane,
nascondimi quello ch'è morto!
Ch'io veda soltanto la siepe
    dell'orto,
la mura ch'ha piene le crepe
    di valeriane.

Nascondi le cose lontane:
le cose son ebbre di pianto!
Ch'io veda i due peschi, i due meli,
    soltanto,
che dànno i soavi lor mieli
    pel nero mio pane.

Fog

Hide what is far from my eyes,
pale fog, impalpable gray
vapor climbing the light
       of the coming day,
after the storm-streaked night,
       the rockfall skies...

Hide what has gone, and what goes,
hide what lies beyond me...
Let me see only that hedge
       at my boundary,
and this wall, by whose crumbling edge
       valerian grows.

Hide from my eyes what is dead:
the world is drunk on tears...
Show my two peach trees in bloom,
       my two pears,
that spread their sugared balm
       on my black bread.

Nascondi le cose lontane
che vogliono ch'ami e che vada!
Ch'io veda là solo quel bianco
    di strada,
che un giorno ho da fare tra stanco
    don don di campane ...

Nascondi le cose lontane,
nascondile, involale al volo
del cuore! Ch'io veda il cipresso
    là, solo,
qui, solo quest'orto, cui presso
    sonnecchia il mio cane.

Hide from my eyes lost things
whose need for my love is a goad...
Let me see only the white
　　　of the stone road—
I too will ride it some night
　　　as a tired bell rings.

Hide the far things—hide
them beyond the sweep of my heart...
Show only that cypress tree,
　　　standing apart,
and here, lying sleepily,
　　　this dog at my side.

La tovaglia

Le dicevano: — Bambina,
che tu non lasci mai stesa,
dalla sera alla mattina,
ma porta dove l'hai presa,
la tovaglia bianca, appena
ch'è terminata la cena!
Bada, che vengono i morti!
i tristi, i pallidi morti!

Entrano, ansimano muti.
Ognuno è tanto mai stanco!
E si fermano seduti
la notte attorno a quel bianco.
Stanno lì sino al domani,
col capo tra le due mani,
senza che nulla si senta,
sotto la lampada spenta. —

È già grande la bambina;
la casa regge, e lavora:
fa il bucato e la cucina,
fa tutto al modo d'allora.
Pensa a tutto, ma non pensa
a sparecchiare la mensa.
Lascia che vengano i morti,
i buoni, i poveri morti.

The Tablecloth

"Dear child," they'd say, "take care
never to leave it spread
on the supper table there
after you've gone to bed,
but put it away again
as soon as supper is done,
lest it invite the dead—
the pale, unhappy dead!

They'll enter, gasping for air.
And each will pass the night,
hunched wearily in a chair,
around that field of white.
Heads in their hands, they'll stay
just so till break of day,
and from this darkened room
no sound at all will come."

That girl is a child no more.
She keeps house, as she must,
as her mother did before:
washes, and cooks, and dusts.
And yet, though perfectly able,
she never clears the table.
She lets them come, the dead,
the kind, unhappy dead.

Oh! la notte nera nera,
di vento, d'acqua, di neve,
lascia ch'entrino da sera,
col loro anelito lieve;
che alla mensa torno torno
riposino fino a giorno,
cercando fatti lontani
col capo tra le due mani.

Dalla sera alla mattina,
cercando cose lontane,
stanno fissi, a fronte china,
su qualche bricia di pane,
e volendo ricordare,
bevono lagrime amare.
Oh! non ricordano i morti,
i cari, i cari suoi morti!

— Pane, sì... pane si chiama,
che noi spezzammo concordi:
ricordate?... È tela, a dama:
ce n'era tanta: ricordi?...
Queste?... Queste sono due,
come le vostre e le tue,
due nostre lagrime amare
cadute nel ricordare! —

Oh! through the darkest black,
through wind or snow or rain,
she lets them come gasping back,
lets them return again
to the table where we sup,
to rest, till the sun comes up,
pursuing some far-off detail,
heads in their hands, and pale.

And so, till morning comes,
they sit, heads bowed, in a ring
and stare at the few stray crumbs
and pursue some far-off thing
down the forgotten years—
but all they find are tears,
for oh! they can't recall them.
Her dear dead can't recall them.

"Bread—yes, that is called bread,
we ate it together, remember?
And that, that's a loose thread,
it makes the cloth, remember?
These? Just a couple of tears,
bitter like yours, and yours,
the usual tears that fall
whenever we recall."

Il gelsomino notturno

E s'aprono i fiori notturni,
nell'ora che penso a' miei cari.
   Sono apparse in mezzo ai viburni
   le farfalle crepuscolari.

Da un pezzo si tacquero i gridi
là sola una casa bisbiglia.
   Sotto l'ali dormono i nidi,
   come gli occhi sotto le ciglia.

Dai calici aperti si esala
l'odore di fragole rosse.
   Splende un lume là nella sala.
   Nasce l'erba sopra le fosse.

Un'ape tardiva sussurra
trovando già prese le celle.
   La Chioccetta per l'aia azzurra
   va col suo pigolio di stelle.

Night-Blooming Jasmine

And in the hour when blooms unfurl
thoughts of my loved ones come to me.
    The moths of evening whirl
    around the snowball tree.

By now no creature barks or sings;
from one house whispers come in rushes.
    Nestlings sleep beneath wings,
    like eyes beneath their lashes.

From the open calyces flows
a ripe strawberry scent, in waves.
    A lamp in the house glows.
    Grasses are born on graves.

A late bee sighs, back from its tours
and no cell vacant anymore.
    The Hen and her cheeping stars
    cross their threshing floor.

Per tutta la notte s'esala
l'odore che passa col vento.
        Passa il lume su per la scala;
        brilla al primo piano: s'è spento...

È l'alba: si chiudono i petali
un poco gualciti; si cova,
        dentro l'urna molle e segreta,
        non so che felicità nuova.

All through the night the flowers flare,
scent flowing and catching the wind.
    The lamp now climbs the stair,
    shines from above, goes dim...

It's dawn: the petals, creased now, shut.
And there, in that soft, secret urn,
    waits some—I know not what—
    new happiness to be born.

L'ora di Barga

Al mio cantuccio, donde non sento
se non le reste brusir del grano,
il suon dell'ore viene col vento
dal non veduto borgo montano:
suono che uguale, che blando cade,
come una voce che persuade.

Tu dici, È l'ora; tu dici, È tardi,
voce che cadi blanda dal cielo.
Ma un poco ancora lascia che guardi
l'albero, il ragno, l'ape, lo stelo,
cose ch'han molti secoli o un anno
o un'ora, e quelle nubi che vanno.

Lasciami immoto qui rimanere
fra tanto moto d'ale e di fronde;
e udire il gallo che da un podere
chiama, e da un altro l'altro risponde,
e, quando altrove l'anima è fissa,
gli strilli d'una cincia che rissa.

The Bells of Barga

Into this nook of mine, where I can hear
only the whisper of the bearded wheat,
the sound of hours blows in on the air
from the unseen village on its mountain seat:
a sound that falls—evenly, placidly—
like a persuasive voice addressing me.

You say, *The time has come.* You say, *It's late,*
O voice that's falling placid from the sky.
But let me look a little longer at
the tree, the stalk, the spider, and the fly—
things that are given centuries or a year,
an hour. Those clouds about to disappear...

Let me remain unmoving a while more
amid the bustle of the wings and branches;
let me hear the crow of a rooster soar
over the fields, the crow of one that answers,
and, with my soul fixed on some other thing,
the squawks of a nearby sparrow bickering.

E suona ancora l'ora, e mi manda
prima un suo grido di meraviglia
tinnulo, e quindi con la sua blanda
voce di prima parla e consiglia,
e grave grave grave m'incuora:
mi dice, È tardi; mi dice, È l'ora.

Tu vuoi che pensi dunque al ritorno,
voce che cadi blanda dal cielo!
Ma bello è questo poco di giorno
che mi traluce come da un velo!
Lo so ch'è l'ora, lo so ch'è tardi;
ma un poco ancora lascia che guardi.

Lascia che guardi dentro il mio cuore,
lascia ch'io viva del mio passato;
se c'è sul bronco sempre quel fiore,
s'io trovi un bacio che non ho dato!
Nel mio cantuccio d'ombra romita
lascia ch'io pianga su la mia vita!

E suona ancora l'ora, e mi squilla
due volte un grido quasi di cruccio,
e poi, tornata blanda e tranquilla,
mi persuade nel mio cantuccio:
è tardi! è l'ora! Sì, ritorniamo
dove son quelli ch'amano ed amo.

Again the hour sounds, first sending me
a pealing bellow of astonishment,
and then, in its previous voice, placidly
speaking to me, advising me, intent
on grave, grave matters I must take to heart:
It's late, it says; *It's time*, it says, *to start.*

You want me, then, to think of the return,
O voice that's falling placid from the sky?
And yet the remnants of this day, which burn
through me as through a veil, delight my eye.
I know it's time, I know it's late—I know.
But let me look a while before I go.

And let me look into my heart this hour,
look back into the past on which I live.
Perhaps that gnarled branch still bears its flower?
Perhaps I'll find a kiss I didn't give?
Here in the shade of my secluded nook,
let me mourn all of this—my life!—and look.

Again the hour sounds: but now it shrieks
two times, each a distressed, distressing cry—
and then, as I sit listening, it speaks
calmly again, persuasive, from the sky:
It's late! It's time! Yes, let's return to see
the ones who love me and are loved by me.

La mia sera

Il giorno fu pieno di lampi;
ma ora verranno le stelle,
le tacite stelle. Nei campi
c'è un breve gre gre di ranelle.
Le tremule foglie dei pioppi
trascorre una gioia leggiera.
Nel giorno, che lampi! che scoppi!
Che pace, la sera!

Si devono aprire le stelle
nel cielo sì tenero e vivo.
Là, presso le allegre ranelle,
singhiozza monotono un rivo.
Di tutto quel cupo tumulto,
di tutta quell'aspra bufera,
non resta che un dolce singulto
nell'umida sera.

È, quella infinita tempesta,
finita in un rivo canoro.
Dei fulmini fragili restano
cirri di porpora e d'oro.
O stanco dolore, riposa!
La nube nel giorno più nera
fu quella che vedo più rosa
nell'ultima sera.

My Evening

The day was full of lightning,
but now the stars will come,
the quiet stars. The frogs
croak briefly in the fields.
A gentle joy blows through
the trembling leaves of poplars.
By day, what flares, what claps!
What peace at evening.

Surely the stars will bloom
in that tender, living sky.
There by the cheerful frogs
a stream is softly sobbing.
Of all the dark upheaval
of all that bitter storm,
no sound but that remains
in the damp evening.

And so the endless storm
ends in the song of a stream.
The fragile bolts have left
cirrus of crimson and gold.
O weary sorrows, rest!
The daytime's darkest cloud
has turned to brightest rose
in the late evening.

Che voli di rondini intorno!
che gridi nell'aria serena!
La fame del povero giorno
prolunga la garrula cena.
La parte, sì piccola, i nidi
nel giorno non l'ebbero intera.
Né io... e che voli, che gridi,
mia limpida sera!

Don... Don... E mi dicono, Dormi!
mi cantano, Dormi! sussurrano,
Dormi! bisbigliano, Dormi!
là, voci di tenebra azzurra...
Mi sembrano canti di culla,
che fanno ch'io torni com'era...
sentivo mia madre... poi nulla...
sul far della sera.

Such flights of swallows swirling!
Such cries on the calm air!
The hunger of the poor day
prolongs their garrulous supper.
The nestlings' daily portion,
though small, is incomplete—
like mine. What flights, what cries,
in my bright evening!

The bells are ringing: *sleep!*
they say. They sing, they murmur,
they whisper to me: *sleep!*
These voices of blue shadows...
they take me, like lullabies,
back to what once I was...
I'd hear my mother, then nothing,
in the dark evening.

Diario autunnale (II)

Per il viale, neri lunghi stormi,
facendo tutto a man a man più fosco,
passano: preti, nella nebbia informi,
che vanno in riga a San Michele in Bosco.

Vanno. Tra loro parlano di morte.
Cadono sopra loro foglie morte.

Sono con loro morte foglie sole.
Vanno a guardare l'agonia del sole.

Autumn Evening

Bologna, 1907

Up the steep road they go, a long black flock,
dimming the air they travel slowly through:
the priests, shapeless in the fog, who walk
to San Michele in Bosco for the view.

They walk, and speak among themselves of death.
And all around them dead leaves fall to earth.

Among them fall the dead leaves, one by one.
They go to watch the death-throes of the sun.

from *Primi poemetti*

Il bordone

Si tagliò da una siepe—era un mattino
triste ma dolce—il suo bordone, e, volta
la fronte, mosse per il suo cammino.

Sì: mosse. E quella era la siepe folta
d'un camposanto, ed era il camposanto,
quello, dove sua madre era sepolta.

D'allora ha errato. Seco avea soltanto
il suo bordone. E qua tese la mano,
e qua la porse. E ha gioito e pianto.

E vide il fiume, il mare, il monte, il piano:
tutto: e a tutto era più presso il cuore
di quanto il piede n'era più lontano.

Disperò sui tramonti, e su le aurore
sperò; sì che la via sempre riprese.
Vuoto era il frutto, ma soave il fiore.

Sopra la soglia d'infinite chiese
pregò. Vide infiniti uomini: alcuno,
Raca! gli disse, ed altri, Ave gli rese:

The Staff

He cut it from a hedge—the breaking day
sad but not cold—and turning, he began
to move. And moving, he was on his way.

It was a hedge beside a cemetery:
the cemetery where his mother lay.
He's wandered ever since. Nothing to carry

except that staff. Has both rejoiced and wept.
Has seen river and sea, mountain and prairie.
The places that were farthest off he kept

closest to heart. At times he lent a hand,
at times was given one. At dusk despaired;
at dawn awoke with hope enough to stand

and carry on. The fruit was empty but
the flower sweet. At countless churches prayed.
Met countless men: some called him idiot,

some wished him well. Each of them drifted by,
like black cloud shadows past a black cloud shadow
on a brown lake. He was what met his eye,

scòrsero i più, come su lago bruno
ombra di nube nera presso nera
ombra di nube. E fu tutto e nessuno.

Sì ch'ora è stanco. Ed è, ora, una sera
triste ma dolce. E sta, come una volta,
presso una siepe. E questa è ancor com'era.

Ché fermo è là, presso la siepe folta
d'un camposanto; e questo camposanto
è quello dove è sua madre sepolta.

Egli è quel ch'era, ma il suo corpo è franto
dall'error lungo; e nel suo cuore è vano
ciò che gioì, ma piange ciò che ha pianto.

E sta, vecchio e canuto, con la mano
sul bordone d'allora. Ed ecco, vede
che da quel giorno radicò pian piano,

il suo bordone, e che visse, e che diede
già fiori e foglie: sotto le sue dita
germinò, radicò sotto il suo piede.

E gli resta una foglia inaridita
che trema. E il vento soffia. E il pellegrino,
curvo sopra la immobile sua vita,

par che muova ora, per il suo cammino.

was no one. Now he's tired. The evening rises,
sad but not cold. He stands there, as before,
beside a hedge. The hedge is as it was.

He stands beside the hedge, unmoving there,
beside the graveyard where his mother lies.
He's what he was, though now in disrepair

from all his wandering, stripped of his glees
but not his griefs. He stands, now white of hair,
hand on the same old staff. And now he sees

that through the years and by degrees his staff
had sent down roots, had been alive, had sprouted
leaves and had bloomed: here where his fingers chafe

it had bloomed; where his feet stand it had rooted.
A withered leaf's the last thing to remain.
It trembles. Wind is blowing. The pilgrim, stooped

over his still life, seems to be moving again.

Digitale purpurea

I.

Siedono. L'una guarda l'altra. L'una
esile e bionda, semplice di vesti
e di sguardi; ma l'altra, esile e bruna,

l'altra... I due occhi semplici e modesti
fissano gli altri due ch'ardono. «E mai
non ci tornasti?» «Mai!» «Non le vedesti

più?» «Non più, cara.» «Io sì: ci ritornai;
e le rividi le mie bianche suore,
e li rivissi i dolci anni che sai;

quei piccoli anni così dolci al cuore...»
L'altra sorrise. «E di': non lo ricordi
quell'orto chiuso? i rovi con le more?

i ginepri tra cui zirlano i tordi?
i bussi amari? quel segreto canto
misterioso, con quel fiore, *fior di*...?»

«*morte*: sì, cara». «Ed era vero? Tanto
io ci credeva che non mai, Rachele,
sarei passata al triste fiore accanto.

Digitalis Purpurea

I.

They sit, each looking at the other. One
is slim and blonde, simple in both her manner
and dress. Ah, but the other, slim and brown,

the other... Two eyes, plain and modest, peer
into the ardent pair. "And so you never
went back? Not even once?" "Never, my dear."

"Well, I did go, and saw them all again,
my sisters in white, and I relived those years,
those sweet years you recall, that little span

I cherished so..." (The other smiles.) "Say,
remember that closed garden? the blackberries?
the junipers full of thrushes, chirping away?

the bitter boxwoods? that strange, secret chant,
about that flower, *bloom of*" — "*death*. Yes, dear,
I do." "And was it true, about its scent?

I thought it was, Rachele, and wouldn't dare
go near those melancholy blooms. They said
their sweet and savage fragrance drugged the air,

Ché si diceva: il fiore ha come un miele
che inebria l'aria; un suo vapor che bagna
l'anima d'un oblìo dolce e crudele.

Oh! quel convento in mezzo alla montagna
cerulea!» Maria parla: una mano
posa su quella della sua compagna;

e l'una e l'altra guardano lontano.

II.

Vedono. Sorge nell'azzurro intenso
del ciel di maggio il loro monastero,
pieno di litanie, pieno d'incenso.

Vedono; e si profuma il lor pensiero
d'odor di rose e di viole a ciocche,
di sentor d'innocenza e di mistero.

E negli orecchi ronzano, alle bocche
salgono melodie, dimenticate,
là, da tastiere appena appena tocche...

Oh! quale vi sorrise oggi, alle grate,
ospite caro? onde più rosse e liete
tornaste alle sonanti camerate

that breathing it dipped your spirit in a fountain
of forgetting." Thus Maria reminisced on
that convent sitting on its sky-blue mountain,

her hand upon her friend's, their gazes distant.

II.

They see. Their convent, set against the blue
of May, arises, full of litanies
and incense smoke. They see, and all they view

is redolent of the violet and the rose—
the scents of innocence and mystery.
And in their ears, and to their lips, there flows

forgotten music, a thrumming run and trill
of keys that had been touched but lightly, lightly...
Oh! what dear visitor smiled across the grille

at you today? for which you went back gladder
and redder to the echoing dormitories today—
for which the *Ave* today is louder,

oggi: ed oggi, più alto, *Ave*, ripete,
Ave Maria, la vostra voce in coro;
e poi d'un tratto (perché mai?) piangete...

Piangono, un poco, nel tramonto d'oro,
senza perché. Quante fanciulle sono
nell'orto, bianco qua e là di loro!

Bianco e ciarliero. Ad or ad or, col suono
di vele al vento, vengono. Rimane
qualcuna, e legge in un suo libro buono.

In disparte da loro agili e sane,
una spiga di fiori, anzi di dita
spruzzolate di sangue, dita umane,

l'alito ignoto spande di sua vita.

III.

«Maria!» «Rachele!» Un poco più le mani
si premono. In quell'ora hanno veduto
la fanciullezza, i cari anni lontani.

Memorie (l'una sa dell'altra al muto
premere) dolci, come è tristo e pio
il lontanar d'un ultimo saluto!

Ave Maria, voices in unison,
and then you suddenly (but why?) are crying...
They cry in the gold light of the late sun,

softly, for no good reason. So many girls—
the garden's white with them! Chatty and white.
They drift in, with a sound like wind-whipped sails.

Some sit alone, to read from some good book.
Apart from the nimble, healthy girls, a sheaf
of blooms, like fingers, bloody ones, that look

human, secretes the strange breath of its life.

III.

"Maria!" "Rachele!" Firmer now their hands
are clasped. For in this hour they have seen
their childhoods: those remote beloved lands.

Sweet memories (the one can tell they're sweet
from the other's grip), the way the fading of
a last goodbye stirs sadness and regret.

«Maria!» «Rachele!» Questa piange, «Addio!»
dice tra sé, poi volta la parola
grave a Maria, ma i neri occhi no: «Io,»

mormora, «sì: sentii quel fiore. Sola
ero con le cetonie verdi. Il vento
portava odor di rose e di viole a

ciocche. Nel cuore, il languido fermento
d'un sogno che notturno arse e che s'era
all'alba, nell'ignara anima, spento.

Maria, ricordo quella grave sera.
L'aria soffiava luce di baleni
silenzïosi. M'inoltrai leggiera,

cauta, su per i molli terrapieni
erbosi. I piedi mi tenea la folta
erba. Sorridi? E dirmi sentia: Vieni!

Vieni! E fu molta la dolcezza! molta!
tanta, che, vedi... (l'altra lo stupore
alza degli occhi, e vede ora, ed ascolta

con un suo lungo brivido...) si muore!»

"Maria!" "Rachele!" And now Rachele cries,
says absently, "Farewell!," then, to Maria,
repeats the weighty word, with distant eyes.

"I did," she murmurs, "smell that flower. There
I was one day, alone with the green beetles.
The scent of rose and violet filled the air.

And in my heart, the slow ferment of all
the dreams that burned at night and with the dawn,
in my blind soul, went out. Yes, I recall

that evening. Silent lightning lit the wind.
I drew near, cautious, slow, the soft deep lawn
clutching my feet. You're smiling? A voice crooned:

Come! Come! Maria, it was sweet! And how!
So sweet that, as you see"—(a sudden startle
widens Maria's eyes, who does see now,

and hears, and shudders at the words)— "it's fatal!"

La quercia caduta

Dov'era l'ombra, or sé la quercia spande
morta, né più coi turbini tenzona.
La gente dice: Or vedo: era pur grande!

Pendono qua e là dalla corona
i nidietti della primavera.
Dice la gente: Or vedo: era pur buona!

Ognuno loda, ognuno taglia. A sera
ognuno col suo grave fascio va.
Nell'aria, un pianto... d'una capinera

che cerca il nido che non troverà.

The Fallen Oak

Where its shade was, the oak itself now sprawls,
lifeless, no longer vying with the wind.
The people say: *I see now—it was tall!*

The little nests of springtime now depend
from limbs that used to rise to a safer height.
People say: *I see now—it was a friend!*

Everyone praises, everyone cuts. Twilight
comes and they haul their heavy loads away.
Then, on the air, a cry—a blackcap in flight,

seeking the nest it will not find today.

L'aquilone

C'è qualcosa di nuovo oggi nel sole,
anzi d'antico: io vivo altrove, e sento
che sono intorno nate le viole.

Son nate nella selva del convento
dei cappuccini, tra le morte foglie
che al ceppo delle quercie agita il vento.

Si respira una dolce aria che scioglie
le dure zolle, e visita le chiese
di campagna, ch'erbose hanno le soglie:

un'aria d'altro luogo e d'altro mese
e d'altra vita: un'aria celestina
che regga molte bianche ali sospese...

sì, gli aquiloni! È questa una mattina
che non c'è scuola. Siamo usciti a schiera
tra le siepi di rovo e d'albaspina.

Le siepi erano brulle, irte; ma c'era
d'autunno ancora qualche mazzo rosso
di bacche, e qualche fior di primavera

The Kite

There's something new under the sun today,
or perhaps ancient: I live here, but feel
violets around me sprouting far away.

They sprout in the forest of the Capuchin monks,
among the dead leaves that leap up and fall
in the spring wind around the great oak trunks.

It's air that comes, fragrant and mild, to thaw
hard dirt, then visit a country church or two
where grass grows green up to the very door:

air that comes from another place and time,
another life: a gust of brilliant blue
up which a scattering of white wings climb...

Ah yes—the kites! And school is out this morning,
and troops of us have picked our various ways
through hedges of blackberry and of hawthorn.

The hedges bristled, withered—though there were,
left over from the fall, a few red sprays
of berries, and here and there a white spring flower.

bianco; e sui rami nudi il pettirosso
saltava, e la lucertola il capino
mostrava tra le foglie aspre del fosso.

Or siamo fermi: abbiamo in faccia Urbino
ventoso: ognuno manda da una balza
la sua cometa per il ciel turchino.

Ed ecco ondeggia, pencola, urta, sbalza,
risale, prende il vento; ecco pian piano
tra un lungo dei fanciulli urlo s'inalza.

S'inalza; e ruba il filo dalla mano,
come un fiore che fugga su lo stelo
esile, e vada a rifiorir lontano.

S'inalza; e i piedi trepidi e l'anelo
petto del bimbo e l'avida pupilla
e il viso e il cuore, porta tutto in cielo.

Più su, più su: già come un punto brilla
lassù lassù... Ma ecco una ventata
di sbieco, ecco uno strillo alto... —Chi strilla?

Sono le voci della camerata
mia: le conosco tutte all'improvviso,
una dolce, una acuta, una velata...

A redbreast robin hopped among the bare
brambles; a lizard from its leaf-muck crevice
poked a small head. And now we're standing there:

Urbino before us, windy; each of us
launching a comet up into the heavens,
to waver, lurch, stall and plummet, then suss

the winds again—and bit by bit to rise,
slowly, amid the long unfurling cheers
of children, until it soars across blue skies.

It soars: and the string slips through the child's hand
like a flower that rises with its stem and veers
away, to bloom again in some far land.

It soars: and with it rises ever higher
the anxious feet, the avid panting chest
and heart, and the wide eyes of the kite-flier.

And higher still: and now it's just a gleam
up there, on high... And then a sudden gust
of crosswind and a scream—but whose, the scream?

I hear, around me, familiar voices speak,
the voices of my friends—I know them all:
the gentle voice, the strident voice, the weak...

A uno a uno tutti vi ravviso,
o miei compagni! e te, sì, che abbandoni
su l'omero il pallor muto del viso.

Sì: dissi sopra te l'orazïoni,
e piansi: eppur, felice te che al vento
non vedesti cader che gli aquiloni!

Tu eri tutto bianco, io mi rammento.
solo avevi del rosso nei ginocchi,
per quel nostro pregar sul pavimento.

Oh! te felice che chiudesti gli occhi
persuaso, stringendoti sul cuore
il più caro dei tuoi cari balocchi!

Oh! dolcemente, so ben io, si muore
la sua stringendo fanciullezza al petto,
come i candidi suoi pètali un fiore

ancora in boccia! O morto giovinetto,
anch'io presto verrò sotto le zolle
là dove dormi placido e soletto...

Meglio venirci ansante, roseo, molle
di sudor, come dopo una gioconda
corsa di gara per salire un colle!

And one by one I recognize each face,
oh my companions! And yes, you're there as well,
your drooping head, your pale averted gaze.

Yes, you, for whom I said my prayers at night
and shed my tears; yet you were lucky, too,
who saw the fall of nothing but a kite.

You were all white, I still recall, but for
the redness of your knees, rubbed raw where you
so often kneeled in prayer on the floor.

Oh, lucky boy, who closed your eyes to rest
with faith still in them, clutching in your fist
the dearest of all the playthings you possessed.

Oh, gently, as I now know all too well,
we die clutching our childhood to our breast,
as flowers hold white petals tight while still

in bud. Oh, little friend who died, I'll soon
be going down beneath the hard dirt too,
down there where you sleep placid and alone...

Better to show up pink-cheeked, out of breath,
and all awash in sweat, like a boy who
just raced his best friend up a hillside path.

Meglio venirci con la testa bionda,
che poi che fredda giacque sul guanciale,
ti pettinò co' bei capelli a onda

tua madre... adagio, per non farti male.

Better to show up with your hair still blond,
combed slowly into lovely waves, which lay
cold on your pillow, by your mother's hand—

combed slowly, so as not to cause you pain.

Nella nebbia

E guardai nella valle: era sparito
tutto! sommerso! Era un gran mare piano,
grigio, senz'onde, senza lidi, unito.

E c'era appena, qua e là, lo strano
vocìo di gridi piccoli e selvaggi:
uccelli spersi per quel mondo vano.

E alto, in cielo, schèletri di faggi,
come sospesi, e sogni di rovìne
e di silenzïosi eremitaggi.

Ed un cane uggiolava senza fine,
né seppi donde, forse a certe péste
che sentii, né lontane né vicine;

eco di péste né tarde né preste,
alterne, eterne. E io laggiù guardai:
nulla ancora e nessuno, occhi, vedeste.

Chiesero i sogni di rovine: «Mai
non giungerà?» Gli scheletri di piante
chiesero: «E tu chi sei, che sempre vai?»

In the Fog

And I stared toward the valley: it was gone—
wholly submerged! A vast flat sea remained,
gray, with no waves, no beaches; all was one.

And here and there I noticed, when I strained,
the alien clamoring of small, wild voices:
birds that had lost their way in that vain land.

And high above, the skeletons of beeches,
as if suspended, and the reveries
of ruins and of the hermit's hidden reaches.

And a dog yelped and yelped, as if in fear,
I knew not where nor why. Perhaps he heard
strange footsteps, neither far away nor near—

echoing footsteps, neither slow nor quick,
alternating, eternal. Down I stared,
but I saw nothing, no one, looking back.

The reveries of ruins asked: "Will no
one come?" The skeletons of trees inquired:
"And who are you, forever on the go?"

Io, forse, un'ombra vidi, un'ombra errante
con sopra il capo un largo fascio. Vidi,
e più non vidi, nello stesso istante.

Sentii soltanto gl'inquïeti gridi
d'uccelli spersi, l'uggiolar del cane,
e, per il mar senz'onde e senza lidi,

le péste né vicine né lontane.

I may have seen a shadow then, an errant
shadow, bearing a bundle on its head.
I saw—and no more saw, in the same instant.

All I could hear were the uneasy screeches
of the lost birds, the yelping of the stray,
and, on that sea that lacked both waves and beaches,

the footsteps, neither near nor far away.

from *Poemi conviviali*

Il sonno di Odisseo

I.

Per nove giorni, e notte e dì, la nave
nera filò, ché la portava il vento
e il timoniere, e ne reggeva accorta
la grande mano d'Odisseo le scotte;
né, lasso, ad altri le cedea, ché verso
la cara patria lo portava il vento.
Per nove giorni, e notte e dì, la nera
nave filò, né l'occhio mai distolse
l'eroe, cercando l'isola rupestre
tra il cilestrino tremolìo del mare;
pago se prima di morir vedesse
balzarne in aria i vortici del fumo.
Nel decimo, là dove era vanito
il nono sole in un barbaglio d'oro,
ora gli apparse non sapea che nero:
nuvola o terra? E gli balenò vinto
dall'alba dolce il grave occhio: e lontano
s'immerse il cuore d'Odisseo nel sonno.

The Sleep of Odysseus

I.

For nine days, night and day, the black
ship scudded, guided by the wind
and by the helmsman's hand, as shrewd
Odysseus worked the sheets. Though weary,
he did not yield them, for the wind
bore him toward his beloved homeland.
For nine days, day and night, the black
ship scudded, the hero's gaze unswerving,
seeking his rocky isle out there
amid that rippling blue—content
could he but glimpse, before he died,
the hearth-smoke coiling to the skies.
On the tenth day, where the ninth sun
had vanished in a blaze of gold,
he saw some sort of blackish shape:
dark cloud or land? But the sweet dawn
pulled down his heavy lids, and the distant
heart of Odysseus plunged into sleep.

II.

E venne incontro al volo della nave,
ecco, una terra, e veleggiava azzurra
tra il cilestrino tremolìo del mare;
e con un monte ella prendea del cielo,
e giù dal monte spumeggiando i botri
scendean tra i ciuffi dell'irsute stipe;
e ne' suoi poggi apparvero i filari
lunghi di viti, ed a' suoi piedi i campi
vellosi della nuova erba del grano:
e tutta apparve un'isola rupestre,
dura, non buona a pascere polledri,
ma sì di capre e sì di buoi nutrice:
e qua e là sopra gli aerei picchi
morian nel chiaro dell'aurora i fuochi
de' mandrïani; e qua e là sbalzava
il mattutino vortice del fumo,
d'Itaca, alfine: ma non già lo vide
notando il cuore d'Odisseo nel sonno.

II.

And square in the path of the fast ship,
sailing to meet them through the trembling
turquoise sea, was a blue land.
Its peak was filling in the sky,
and plunging down from it ravines
bristled and foamed with tufts of scrub,
and over its foothills ran long rows
of vines, and at its feet lay fields
furred by the stalks of the new wheat.
And all the isle seemed rugged and hard,
poor for the pasturing of foals
but good for goats and fine for oxen,
and here and there on lofty peaks
the herdsmen's fires in the light of dawn
were dying out, and here and there
the coils of hearth-smoke rose, at last,
from Ithaca—but rose unseen:
the heart of Odysseus swam in sleep.

III.

Ed ecco a prua dell'incavata nave
volar parole, simili ad uccelli,
con fuggevoli sibili. La nave
radeva allora il picco alto del Corvo
e il ben cerchiato fonte; e se n'udiva
un grufolare fragile di verri;
ed ampio un chiuso si scorgea, di grandi
massi ricinto ed assiepato intorno
di salvatico pero e di prunalbo;
ed il divino mandrïan dei verri,
presso la spiaggia, della nera scorza
spogliava con l'aguzza ascia un querciolo,
e grandi pali a rinforzare il chiuso
poi ne tagliò coi morsi aspri dell'ascia;
e sì e no tra lo sciacquìo dell'onde
giungeva al mare il roco ansar dei colpi,
d'Eumeo fedele: ma non già li udiva
tuffato il cuore d'Odisseo nel sonno.

III.

Then, from the bow of the hollow ship,
the words of his men flew like birds,
with fleeting sibilance. The ship
skirted the dome of Raven Rock
and the well-girt spring; one could hear
the delicate sounds of rooting hogs
and glimpse an ample pen, enclosed
by massive rocks and hedged about
with wild pear trees and hawthorn brake.
And near the shore, with his sharp axe,
the noble herder of those hogs
stripped black bark from a sapling oak
and from it hacked with biting blows
long stakes to strengthen his enclosure.
At times, amid the lapping of waves,
the cough of the axe of faithful Eumaeus
reached the water—but went unheard:
the heart of Odysseus sank in sleep.

IV.

E già da prua, sopra la nave, a poppa,
simili a freccie, andavano parole
con fuggevoli fremiti. La nave
era di faccia al porto di Forkyne;
e in capo ad esso si vedea l'olivo,
grande, fronzuto, e presso quello un antro:
l'antro d'affaccendate api sonoro,
quando in crateri ed anfore di pietra
filano la soave opra del miele:
e si scorgeva la sassosa strada
della città: si distinguea, tra il verde
d'acquosi ontani, la fontana bianca
e l'ara bianca, ed una eccelsa casa:
l'eccelsa casa d'Odisseo: già forse
stridea la spola fra la trama, e sotto
le stanche dita ricrescea la tela,
ampia, immortale... Oh! non udì né vide
perduto il cuore d'Odisseo nel sonno.

IV.

And then, from stem to stern and back,
the words of his men shot like arrows,
with fleeting shivers. Now the ship
was gliding toward the port at Phorcys,
on whose shores grew an olive tree,
massive and leafy, beside a cave
that hummed with the industry of bees,
as they, in bowls and pitchers of stone,
spun the sweet substance of their honey.
And one could see the stony road
leading to town, could glimpse, beyond
the sea-green alders, a white fountain,
and a white altar, and a great house:
Odysseus' house, where even then,
perhaps, beneath tired hands, a shuttle
hissed through a loom, a broad, immortal
fabric regrew... Oh! deaf and blind,
the heart of Odysseus foundered in sleep.

V.

E su la nave, nell'entrare il porto,
il peggio vinse: sciolsero i compagni
gli otri, e la furia ne fischiò dei venti:
la vela si svoltò, si sbatté, come
peplo, cui donna abbandonò disteso
ad inasprire sopra aereo picco:
ecco, e la nave lontanò dal porto;
e un giovinetto stava già nel porto,
poggiato all'asta dalla bronzea punta:
e il giovinetto sotto il glauco olivo
stava pensoso; ed un veloce cane
correva intorno a lui scodinzolando:
e il cane dalle volte irrequïete
sostò, con gli occhi all'infinito mare;
e com'ebbe le salse orme fiutate,
ululò dietro la fuggente nave:
Argo, il suo cane: ma non già l'udiva
tuffato il cuore d'Odisseo nel sonno.

V.

And on his ship, at the port's mouth,
the worst words won: his men unbound
the bag, and the raging winds howled out:
the sail reversed and started flapping
like an outspread house-dress hung
to dry atop some airy peak.
And so the ship sailed out of port,
away from a boy who stood nearby,
leaning upon a bronze-tipped spear
beneath the gray-green olive. The boy
was lost in thought, and a swift dog
was running loops around him, wagging,
but soon its restless circling ceased,
it paused, eyes on the endless sea,
and having sniffed its salty traces
now bayed at the escaping ship:
Argo, his dog—who bayed unheard:
the heart of Odysseus sank in sleep.

VI.

E la nave radeva ora una punta
d'Itaca scabra. E tra due poggi un campo
era, ben culto; il campo di Laerte;
del vecchio re; col fertile pometo;
coi peri e meli che Laerte aveva
donati al figlio tuttavia fanciullo;
ché lo seguiva per la vigna, e questo
chiedeva degli snelli alberi e quello:
tredici peri e dieci meli in fila
stavano, bianchi della lor fiorita:
all'ombra d'uno, all'ombra del più bianco,
era un vecchio, poggiato su la marra:
il vecchio, volto all'infinito mare
dove mugghiava il subito tumulto,
limando ai faticati occhi la luce,
riguardò dietro la fuggente nave:
era suo padre: ma non già lo vide
notando il cuore d'Odisseo nel sonno.

VI.

And now the ship rounded a headland,
and there, between two rugged hills,
lay thriving orchards of pear and apple,
well tended: the orchards of Laertes,
orchards the old king had bestowed
upon his son when his son was a boy
and liked to trail him asking this
or that about the slender trees—
ten apple trees and thirteen pears,
in rows, trees white with blossoms now.
And in the shade of one, the whitest,
an old man leaned against his hoe,
facing the endless sea on which
a sudden storm had begun to howl.
Shielding his tired eyes from the light,
he watched a ship as it raced away.
But father was yet unseen by son,
for the heart of Odysseus swam in sleep.

VII.

Ed i venti portarono la nave
nera più lungi. E subito aprì gli occhi
l'eroe, rapidi aprì gli occhi a vedere
sbalzar dalla sognata Itaca il fumo;
e scoprir forse il fido Eumeo nel chiuso
ben cinto, e forse il padre suo nel campo
ben culto: il padre che sopra la marra
appoggiato guardasse la sua nave;
e forse il figlio che poggiato all'asta
la sua nave guardasse: e lo seguiva,
certo, e intorno correa scodinzolando
Argo, il suo cane; e forse la sua casa,
la dolce casa ove la fida moglie
già percorreva il garrulo telaio:
guardò: ma vide non sapea che nero
fuggire per il violaceo mare,
nuvola o terra? e dileguar lontano,
emerso il cuore d'Odisseo dal sonno.

VII.

And the winds carried the black ship
far from the shore. And the hero's eyes
opened then, hoping to see smoke
leap from the Ithaca he'd dreamed of;
hoping to glimpse faithful Eumaeus
tending his swine, or maybe his father
in his tidy orchard—his father who,
gripping a hoe, was watching his ship;
or maybe his son, gripping a spear
and watching too. Or Argo his dog,
running in circles, wagging his tail
and watching—maybe even his own
sweet home, in which his faithful wife
plied her garrulous loom... He looked,
but all he saw was a blackish shape—
dark cloud or land?—escaping over
the violet sea and melting away
as the heart of Odysseus rose from sleep.

Il remo confitto

E per nove anni al focolar sedeva,
di sua casa, l'Eroe navigatore:
ché più non gli era alcuno error marino
dal fato ingiunto e alcuno error terrestre.
Sì, la vecchiaia gli ammollia le membra
a poco a poco. Ora dovea la morte
fuori del mare giungergli, soave,
molto soave, e né coi dolci strali
dovea ferirlo, ma fiatar leggiera
sopra la face cui già l'uragano
frustò, ma fece divampar più forte.
E i popoli felici erano intorno,
che il figlio, nato lungi alle battaglie,
savio reggeva in abbondevol pace.
Crescean nel chiuso del fedel porcaio
floridi i verri dalle bianche zanne,
e nei ristretti pascoli più tanti
erano i bovi dalle larghe fronti,
e tante più dal Nerito le capre
pendean strappando irsuti pruni e stipe,
e molto sotto il tetto alto giaceva
oro, bronzo, olezzante olio d'oliva.

The Fixed Oar

And for nine years he sat beside the hearth
of his own house: the navigator Hero,
no longer forced by fate to wander by sea,
to wander by land. His limbs, of course, with age,
had slowly softened. Death would come for him
out of the sea, but gently, gently, not
by wounding him with its sweet arrows but
by breathing lightly on the torch that gales
had often whipped, making it burn the brighter.
And all around him a happy population,
ruled, by a son born far from war, with wisdom
and in abundant peace. The white-tusked boars
grew fatter in the faithful swineherd's pen,
the broad-head oxen swelled the narrow pastures,
and goats bedecked the slopes of Neriton,
tearing the shaggy brush, the thorny scrub,
while far below, beneath the tallest roof,
lay gold, lay bronze, lay fragrant olive oil.
Yet feasts were hosted seldom in that house:
no merry din now filled the great dark halls,
for the old man no longer craved the steak,
no longer craved the fatty ham; he longed,

Ma raro nella casa era il convito,
né più sonava l'ilare tumulto
per il grande atrio umbratile; ché il vecchio
più non bramava terghi di giovenco,
né coscie gonfie d'adipe, di verro;
amava, invano, la fioril vivanda,
il dolce loto, cui chi mangia, è pago,
né altro chiede che brucar del loto.
Così le soglie dell'eccelsa casa
or d'Odissèo dimenticò l'aedo
dai molti canti, e il lacero pitocco,
che l'un corrompe e l'altro orna il convito.
E il Laertiade ora vivea solingo
fuori del mare, come il vecchio remo
scabro di salsa gromma, che piantato
lungi avea dalle salse aure nel suolo,
e strettolo, ala, tra le glebe gravi.
E il grigio capo dell'Eroe tremava,
avanti al mormorare della fiamma,
come là, nella valle solitaria,
quel remo al soffio della tramontana.

in vain, to live on flowers: on the sweet lotus,
whose eater is content and asks for nothing
more than to graze on lotus blooms forever.
Thus both the bard, who graces a feast with song,
and the beggar, who defiles it with his rags,
forgot the halls of the high house of Odysseus.
Laertes' son now lived as if alone,
out of the sea, like the old oar he had planted
in dry earth, far from any salty breeze—
that wing, crusted with salt, clutched by hard clods.
And the gray-haired Hero trembled as the flame
murmured, just as that oar, in its lonely valley,
shook when the cold wind from the mountains blew.

Uncollected Poems

Voci misteriose

La nebbia gemica, tira una buffa
ch'empie di foglie stridule il fosso;
lieve nell'arida siepe si tuffa
    il pettirosso;

sotto la nebbia vibra il vocale
canneto un brivido quasi febbrile;
sopra la nebbia lontano sale
    il campanile;

passo, e precedemi sul limo un gaio
stormo di passeri quasi irridendo,
mentr'io nel plumbeo ciel di gennaio
    l'orecchio tendo.

Tendo l'orecchio nel faticato
di pensier torbido cielo d'inverno,
in cui forse Eschilo meditò il fato,
    Dante, l'inferno,

Mysterious Voices

The fog distills, the cold wind gushes,
filling the gully with rasping leaves;
gracefully through the withered bushes
          a robin weaves.

Beneath the fog the cane field seems
to murmur with a fevered tremor;
above the fog, far off, there looms
          the old bell tower.

A crowd of January sparrows
laughs on the muddy path ahead
as I forge on, darkened by shadows,
          by clouds of lead,

ear to that thought-worn sky, whose fit
of murky wintry gloom might well
tempt Aeschylus to ponder fate,
          or Dante, hell—

in cui la pallida strega—e i ghiacciai
con rombe assidue rompeansi a tratti—
dubitò il termine venuto omai
                    scritto ne' patti.

Come la pallida strega, l'orecchio
tendo, anch'io, pallido, d'antichi
eventi a voci e strepiti, che il mondo vecchio
                    canta tra i venti.

Non è la nebbia che per la piana
via le pozzanghere trepida batte,
ma là tra l'aere dubbio una strana
                    voce combatte:

pari d'Eolie lire al concento
nell'Apollinee splendide gare,
nuova Olimpiade sui monti sento
                    rumoreggiare.

Un grido fervido, lungo, echeggiante
Pan manda il postumo, Pan che non muore,
Pan per le cedue boscaglie errante
                    Dio vincitore.

might cause the pallid witch to doubt
(as glaciers, with long groans, have cracked)
the payment-due date written out
                  on a tattered pact.

I, like the witch, am pale with old
ordeals, and my ears too attend
to the voices and noises the ancient world
                  sings in the wind.

It's not the skittish mists that craze
the puddles along my level alley;
rather I hear, in the higher haze,
                  a strange voice rally:

the peer of a chorus of wind harps,
Apollo's rival, with equal skills...
A new Olympiad's flats and sharps
                  sound in the hills.

A cry that echoes, long and ardent,
through time: Pan in the deep wood,
the copse... Pan: the undying, errant,
                  triumphant God.

Il ritorno

«Tua madre» mi scrivono un giorno
«sta male... sta peggio» poi... «muore».
Su rapide rote io ritorno.

È pallida l'aria; ne cade
la pioggia con stroscie sonore:
son tutta una pozza le strade.

«Non parla, non vede» a la porta
mi dicono «più! né baciarla
puoi più che in un viso di morta
                    già freddo!»

M'accosto al suo letto: ella un poco
li occhi alza: ella vede, ella parla:
«Oh, povero bimbo!... del fuoco,
                    che ha freddo!»

The Return

"Your mother," says the letter,
"is very ill"—and then:
"she's getting worse, not better."

A carriage speeds me back.
Rain makes the road a fen.
Thunderheads flash and crack.

"She cannot see, or speak,"
I'm told when I arrive.
"And if you kiss her cheek,
        you'll find it cold."

As I approach, her lids
flicker and lift—alive!
"Quick, make a fire," she bids,
        "my poor boy's cold!"

My Pascoli

"He came after Homer and before Gertrude
Stein, a difficult interval for a poet."
—Anne Carson

*P*ascoli's childhood was famously tragic: his father was shot to
death when he was eleven (a murder that was never solved), his
mother and oldest sister died the following year, and two of his
brothers were dead by the time he was twenty. I mention these
facts here not because I want you to bear them in mind as you
read the poems, but rather to get them out of the way. In Italy
the dramas of his life are so notorious (as, in English, with Oscar
Wilde, say, or Sylvia Plath) that they have congealed into a sort
of durable myth that sometimes overshadows and distorts the
work.[1] Even when Pascoli's poems themselves evoke or allude
to his tragic personal history, they are often better served, in my
view, by considering them more narrowly, independent of that
history, or else more broadly, within the larger context of fin
de siècle Italian poetry, which, with Pascoli's help, was tilting
toward modernity.

---

1   I do not mean to suggest that his life and work cannot profitably
be considered together, and for anyone who is interested in doing so I highly
recommend starting with *Beyond the Family Romance: The Legend of Pascoli*
(U. of Toronto, 2007) by Maria Truglio, who examines the uncanny qualities
of his poetry and puts his life and work in productive conversation.

Pascoli came—to paraphrase Anne Carson's irresistible remark about Stesichorus—in the difficult interval between Dante and Marinetti. He wrote nearly all his best work in the last decade of the nineteenth century and the first few years of the twentieth, an extraordinary burst that included his three most important volumes of poetry, *Myricae*, *Canti di Castelvecchio*, and *Primi poemetti*—each of which was expanded and reprinted multiple times during those years—as well as three volumes of Dante criticism and a large body of original poetry in Latin. But by 1906, the year he succeeded his dying mentor, Giosuè Carducci, as Professor of Italian Literature at the University of Bologna, his best work was behind him. The real changing of the guard had, in any case, taken place years earlier in the poems themselves: Carducci's marmoreal neoclassicism had given way to his student's plainer, less rhetorical style; the nineteenth century had given way to the twentieth. When Pascoli died in 1912, of cirrhosis, he left behind a major body of innovative work that would cast a long shadow. Gabriele D'Annunzio, the only other fin de siècle poet of comparable importance, called him the greatest Italian poet since Petrarch.

At his best, Pascoli provides what Joseph Cary calls "a rough antithesis or even antidote" to the grandeur, or grandiosity, of the older Carducci and the younger D'Annunzio, and as Robert Dombrowski observes, he "contributed more than any other poet of the time, including D'Annunzio, to the renewal of Italian poetry in the twentieth century." But he remains obscure in English. The sharp disparity between his national and international fortunes has been ascribed,

as such disparities often are, to a vague "untranslatability":
Cesare Garboli, editor of the magnificent Meridiani edition
of Pascoli's selected work (2002), called him "a profoundly
Italian poet [who] isn't easy to translate"; Montale called him
"as untranslatable as Leopardi." Perhaps. But I suspect that
his international neglect may, rather, be largely a function of
historical fashion: he wasn't part of any group or movement,
and his poetic moment was not a glamorous one, especially in
comparison to the radical modernisms, heralded by Marinetti's
Futurist Manifesto in 1909, that were remaking the scene just as
Pascoli was leaving it.

◊

Pascoli is, above all, a poet of memory and a poet of
things. He is known for his poetics of the *fanciullino*, his term
for the innocent, non-rational intuition possessed by children
and poets and associated with lyricism and creativity, and for
his focus on *piccole cose*, small things that constitute the essence
of his world and that he names with a precision new to Italian
poetry. (Where Leopardi, a notoriously inexact naturalist, might
refer generically to "birdsong," Pascoli might name the exact
species or even transcribe its call phonetically, and he famously
scolded Leopardi for putting roses and violets into the same
bouquet in a poem, even though they don't bloom at the same
time.) The title of his first book, *Myricae*, is neatly emblematic

of this aspect of his poetics: taken from a reference by Virgil to *humilesque myricae* (humble tamarisks), it emphasizes the humble object, properly named. It also, of course, emphasizes Pascoli's classical erudition, and yet he believed that the truest poetry arose not from erudition but from a connection to something child-like within, an interior vision that allows the poet to continue to see things as if for the first time. In the following passage from *Il fanciullino*, his most famous articulation of his poetics, he dramatizes this idea:

> In each of us is a small child that not only shivers with fear—as Cebes of Thebes, the first to discover its presence within him, believed—but also sheds tears and feels joys of its own. When we are still very young, its voice is inseparable from ours, and the two children play and vie with each other, always together, fearing and hoping, rejoicing and weeping, with only one heartbeat to be heard between them, one shout, one whimper. But then we grow older and it remains young; a new desire flares in our eyes, but its gaze remains fixed on its perennial serene wonder. Our voice deepens and roughens; its voice goes on chiming like a bell forever—a secret chime that we may hear more clearly when we're older, because in our youth we are busy arguing and pleading our life's case and so are less able to pay attention to the corner of our soul from which it comes. Moreover, the invisible child is shyer with the youth, with whom it finds less common ground, than with the grown man or the old man. The youth, in fact, only rarely and fleetingly deigns to converse with

the child, whose company he avoids, like one embarrassed by his recent past. But the settled man loves talking with it and hearing its chatter and replying in solemn tones, and the harmony of their voices is sweet to hear, like the trill of a nightingale near a murmuring brook. [...] Advancing years do not prevent us from hearing the small voice of the inner child. In fact, in old age, when there is less competing noise, we may be better able to attend to that voice hidden in the soul's shadows. And when the eyes with which the old man looks outside himself begin to fail, well, then he uses only those large internal eyes, seeing nothing before him but the vision that he had as a child, that all children habitually have. When Homer is painted, he should be shown old and blind, with a small child who is always talking and looking about leading him by the hand—a boy or a girl, the god or the goddess: the god who planted all those songs deep in Phemius's heart, or the goddess whom the blind aoidos invoked when he sang of Achilles and Odysseus.

Much of Pascoli's own best work indeed has a kind of wide-eyed interiority that seems to owe as much to an inner child as to an erudite professor.

    This focus on things, and on seeing them with fresh eyes—especially in the fragmentary, image-driven, muted tones of his earlier poems—were new to Italian poetry. To American readers, some of those poems may seem to anticipate Pound's imagism or William Carlos Williams' "no ideas but in things." Though he was clearly no Modernist—and though he himself seemed always to be looking backward, and inward, toward his childhood—his work pointed a way forward, and its influence shaped an important strain of modern Italian poetry. Influence is hard to gauge, of course, but I hear echoes of Pascoli in the work of poets including Umberto Saba, Carlo Betocchi, Eugenio Montale, Sandro Penna, Pier Paolo Pasolini, and many others. Whether or not he is any more "untranslatable" than other great poets, I can think of no other Italian poet who has been so unjustly confined to his own borders.[2]

◊

I should be clear that the slim selection of poems in this volume is a personal and no doubt idiosyncratic one. It does not offer a representative overview of Pascoli's work but rather a particular slice of it—a slice I think of as *my* Pascoli. He was so prolific and diverse that there may be said to be many Pascolis. The least appealing, to me, is the last Pascoli, the "National Pascoli," author of patriotic and historical works such as "Poemi Italici," "Poemi del Risorgimento," and "Le canzoni di Re Enzio." There is also, of course, the "Tragic Pascoli," exemplified by maudlin anthology pieces "X agosto" and "La cavallina storna," both of which engage in obvious ways the events mentioned at the beginning of this introduction. Then there is the "Scholastic Pascoli," which includes his Latin poetry and his fascinating Homerica (especially sequences such as "The Sleep of Odysseus,"

---

2   The injustice is particularly notable in English, given Pascoli's affinity with poets such as Tennyson, Shelley, and Wordsworth (whose "We Are Seven" Pascoli famously translated), and scholars such as James Sully, Herbert Spencer, and Max Müller.

included here in its entirety, and "The Last Voyage," a section of which—"The Fixed Oar"—is included here). "Pastoral Pascoli," in which the natural world takes center stage, is widely appreciated in Italy, and rightly so: he wrote many beautiful nature lyrics, several of which I've included here, in which the poet seems to disappear, becoming merely an eye that dissolves into the landscape it observes.

And then there's my Pascoli, a poet who has written a handful of the most beautiful and wistful poems I know in any language: poems such as "Fog," for example, or "The Bells of Barga," or "Hometown," or "Last Dream," or "Night-Blooming Jasmine." This Pascoli often draws on Pastoral Pascoli, except here a human figure takes center stage. Whether he is wandering or sitting near home, this figure is a kind of thoughtful, haunted pilgrim, whose imagination reaches simultaneously outward, into the natural world around him; backward, into a past where abstract loved ones still abide; and forward, toward his own future death that will, in a way that feels mystical without feeling religious, close the circle with the past. In several poems, fog keeps both the past and the future—all that is unreachable or unknowable or threatening—at bay. (Pascoli's fog is a close cousin to Leopardi's famous hedge, which in the poem "L'infinito" blocks from view the vast, frightening spaces and silences beyond it.)

Strangely, for a poet of his prolificity, there is no "Amorous Pascoli"; he didn't write love poems. He regretted that "modern poets" were "so utterly fixated on love and on women," and his theory of the *fanciullino* posited that erotic or romantic love isn't a great poetic subject because it isn't what matters to that wide-eyed child who leads the poet by the hand. When his poems do touch on sexuality, they do so ambivalently—and florally. In "Digitalis Purpurea," erotic desire is depicted as alluring but dangerous, even deadly—the nunnery seems safer. In "Night-Blooming Jasmine," a strange and gorgeous epithalamion that many consider his greatest poem, the erotic scene (witnessed from afar and displaced onto the titular flower) portends the birth of something new and happy—though the image of an urn where we expect something closer to a womb is, to say the least, unsettling.

In any case, whatever happiness that poem may portend belongs not to the poet but to the friend for whose marriage it was written. Pascoli himself never married, living most of his adult life with his sisters Ida and Maria. Much is made of this odd *ménage* by critics and biographers, who see it as an attempt to restore the shattered familial "nest" of his childhood—a nest that marriage would necessarily rupture. And indeed when Ida married and moved out, in 1895, Pascoli was devastated. He lived the last seventeen years of his life with Maria, who aggressively and successfully sabotaged his own attempted engagement. Once, when an interviewer asked him what his greatest passion was, he replied: "It would be love, but it's smoking."

Geoffrey Brock

ACKNOWLEDGMENTS

For fellowships that helped me finish this book, I would like
to thank the National Endowment for the Arts and Brown
University's George A. and Eliza Gardner Howard Foundation.
I'm also grateful to the editors of the following journals, which
published earlier versions of these translations:

Able Muse: "The Fallen Oak," "November"
Academy of American Poets' Poem-a-Day: "Night-Blooming Jasmine"
The Literary Review: "The Kite"
Mare Nostrum: "Storm"
New Poetry in Translation: "Plowing," "Autumn Evening,"
        "Railway," "Home"
PN Review: "Fog," "Epigrams for Giacinto," "My Evening"
Poetry: "In the Fog," "Last Dream"
Unsplendid: "Night-Blooming Jasmine"
The Yale Review: "The Tablecloth"
Zocalo: "Shearwaters of the Adriatic"

Versions of "November," "Last Dream," "Back Then!," "In the
Fog," and "Night-Blooming Jasmine" also appear in *The FSG
Book of Twentieth-Century Italian Poetry* (Farrar, Straus &
Giroux, 2012)

GIOVANNI PASCOLI (1855-1912) was the greatest Italian poet writing at the beginning of the twentieth century, and he exerted an enormous influence on modern Italian poetry. His chief collections include *Myricae*, *Canti di Castelvecchio*, and *Primi poemetti*.

GEOFFREY BROCK is the author of *Weighing Light* and *Voices Bright Flags*, the editor of *The FSG Book of 20th-Century Italian Poetry*, and the translator of numerous books of Italian poetry and prose. He teaches in the MFA program at the University of Arkansas.

The text of *Last Dream* is set in Garamond Premier Pro.
Cover design by Kyle G. Hunter.